MATT CHRISTOPHER

On the Track with . . .

MATT CHRISTOPHER

On the Track with...
Jeff Gordon

Text by Glenn Stout

Little, Brown and Company
Boston   New York   London

First Edition

Matt Christopher™ is a trademark of Catherine M. Christopher.

Cover photograph by Mary Ann Chastain/Associated Press

Library of Congress Cataloging-in-Publication Data

Stout, Glenn.
    On the track with . . . Jeff Gordon / text by Glenn Stout. — 1st ed.
        p.   cm.
    ISBN 0-316-13469-4
    1. Gordon, Jeff, 1971–   —Juvenile literature.   2. Automobile
racing drivers — United States — Biography — Juvenile literature.
[1. Gordon, Jeff, 1971–   .   2. Automobile racing drivers.]   I. Title: At
head of title: Matt Christopher.   II. Christopher, Matt.   III. Title.
GV1032.G67 S87   2001
796.72'092 — dc21
[B]   00-040544

10 9 8 7 6 5 4 3 2 1

COM-MO

Printed in the United States of America

Contents

MATT CHRISTOPHER

On the Track with...

Chapter One:
1971–1976

Born to Race

Jeff Gordon gets carsick.

That's right. When NASCAR champion Jeff Gordon rides in a car as a passenger, he gets motion sickness. He can't wait to get out of the car.

But when he's on the racetrack, rocketing down the track at more than 200 miles per hours behind the wheel of his car, it's a different story. He feels great. There's nothing he would like to do more.

On the track Gordon is known for his hard-driving style, his will to win, and his unmatched record of success. His performance makes the opposition feel bad, because when Jeff Gordon is in a race the other drivers know they are often competing for the privilege to finish second behind Gordon.

Before he had even learned to walk, Jeff Gordon appeared destined to drive a race car. Gordon was born on August 4, 1971, in Vallejo, California, about twenty-five miles from San Francisco. But when Jeff was only three months old, his mother, Carol, and father, Will Gordon, divorced. Little Jeff and his four-year-old sister, Kim, lived with their mother. The young family was on their own.

Carol Gordon worked for a medical-supply company. In the summer of 1972, just as Jeff was learning to walk, another employee of the company, John Bickford, mustered the courage to ask Carol out on a date. He wasn't put off by the fact that Carol had two small children. He was also divorced and remained very close to his son, who lived with his ex-wife. He understood how important Carol Gordon's children were to her.

Bickford worked adapting vans for use by disabled people. He loved all kinds of automobiles, and if there was one thing he liked better than taking a car apart and putting it back together, it was auto racing. For their first date, John asked Carol if she and her two children would like to attend an auto race on Labor Day at the nearby Vallejo Speedway. Carol readily agreed, and little Jeff Gordon attended his first automobile race while he was still crawling on the ground in diapers.

John Bickford quickly became a frequent visitor to the Gordon home. Jeff and Kim loved the extra attention they received from John, and over the next couple of years John and Carol grew closer. They shared the same dreams. Both wanted to have a family together and make a better life for each other. They soon married, and John became Jeff and Kim's stepfather.

John particularly enjoyed playing with Jeff, and Jeff looked up to John. By the time Jeff was three years old John had taught him how to ride a two-wheel bicycle. Jeff never even owned a tricycle.

Many kids in the neighborhood raced BMX bicycles, small-frame bikes with wide, knobby wheels designed for off-road riding. As soon as Jeff saw the neighborhood children racing their bikes at the BMX track down the street, he wanted a BMX bike, too.

John got Jeff a BMX bike. The young boy had lots of energy, and John thought it was a good idea to give Jeff something constructive to do. But Carol was less than thrilled to see Jeff on the BMX bike. Most of neighborhood kids with BMX bikes were eight or ten years old. Jeff was only four, and she didn't like the idea of little Jeff trying to keep up with kids twice his age and size.

But Jeff Gordon was fearless. He thought nothing of careening as fast as he could down a big hill near their house. He pestered John to let him race, and at only age four he made his BMX bike–racing debut in the sport's youngest division, for kids age eight and under. He was usually the youngest competitor.

He wasn't very successful at first. The other kids were simply bigger and stronger than he was, and he had a hard time keeping up. When Jeff got passed by the other racers or cut off going around a corner, he became frustrated. Then John Bickford had an idea.

After spending all day adapting vans and cars for use by the disabled, he decided to use his skills on Jeff's BMX bike. He created a lightweight bike designed especially for Jeff. The lighter bike and lots of practice made Jeff competitive in the races. He even managed to win a race as a four-year-old, a remarkable accomplishment.

But Carol still worried about her son's safety. Even though racers wore helmets and special padding, at almost every race meet one or two young children wrecked their bikes and had to be taken to the hospital with minor injuries. Although Jeff managed to avoid getting seriously hurt, Carol was still concerned and asked John to stop taking Jeff to the BMX track.

John reluctantly agreed, but he knew Jeff would be disappointed. He had already fallen in love with racing. So John bought two quarter-midget racing cars, a pink one for Jeff's sister and a black one for Jeff. Quarter-midget cars are open-wheeled cars, meaning they have no fenders, designed for racing on dirt tracks by children. They are powered by a small 2.85-horsepower engine and don't go very fast. Safety is the primary consideration of the cars; the driver is protected by a seat belt, a shoulder harness, and a safety roll bar in case the car rolls over. Drivers must always wear helmets, gloves, and special padding.

Carol later told reporters that when John brought the two cars home she thought it was "a pretty crazy idea." But Jeff fell in love with his car instantly, and when John promised that he'd make sure everything was safe, Carol didn't have the heart to ask John to return them. She soon realized that racing the small cars were less dangerous than racing BMX bikes.

But it wasn't legal or safe to drive the cars on the street. Jeff and his sister needed a place to learn to drive. John noticed an empty lot adjacent to a nearby fairground and talked the fairground officials into allowing him to build a regulation, one-fifth-mile, quarter-midget racetrack.

John spent three full days clearing brush and moving dirt around to create the track. As soon as he was finished, Jeff couldn't wait to jump in the car and start driving.

He quickly learned that driving a car, even a very small, slow one, was far different from riding a BMX bike. Cars are much heavier, and on the loose dirt they tend to slip and slide all over the place. At first, Jeff could hardly keep the car on the track.

But each time he skidded off the track or stalled the engine, John trotted over to Jeff and tried to teach him what he had done wrong. Even though the car was small and slow, Jeff had to learn some of the same fundamental lessons of driving that professional NASCAR drivers learn.

He had to learn when to accelerate and when to brake. For example, a driver should accelerate while coming out of a turn. If a driver does so too late, he or she loses speed. But if a driver accelerates too early, the car can slide off the track. Jeff also had to learn to follow what is known as a line, the path around the racetrack that allows the car to go at the highest possible speed without slipping.

Jeff's sister, Kim, soon lost interest in driving her car, but Jeff couldn't get enough of it. When John returned home from work each day, Jeff pestered him into taking him to the track to practice.

Jeff wanted to enter races right away, but Carol still wasn't too anxious to see her son on the track competing against others. John agreed, for he knew that Jeff had a lot of learning to do before it would be safe for him to compete. Jeff practiced for nearly a year before he was allowed to compete in a real race.

Now he was a race-car driver. He was only five years old.

Chapter Two:
1976–1984

The Prodigy

When John came home with Jeff's first racing suit, Jeff beamed. The shiny, sparkly helmet gleamed and had his last name painted on the visor. His racing suit and gloves were miniature versions of those used by professional drivers. When he put them on, Jeff looked like a pro.

Yet despite all his hours of practice at the track, Jeff's driving skills were anything but professional. As a rookie racer, he had to start at the back of the pack. In the heat of the competition of his first race, Jeff got too excited and forgot much of what he had learned. On almost every turn, he accelerated too soon and spun out. He learned that driving by himself on a track was far different from racing against other cars. He hadn't learned how to pick his way through the pack and pass other cars. He was lapped or passed by most of the other drivers. He finished far back in the race.

The other drivers, most of whom were several years older, teased him for being so young and inexperienced. This upset Jeff's mother, and she volunteered to help Jeff learn to race.

John adapted a midget racer for his wife, and during practice sessions at the fairground, she raced against Jeff. He learned how to draft behind her, which cut down the wind resistance on his car, and then slingshot out and charge past her.

The extra practice helped and Jeff improved dramatically. He quickly learned to stay calm and remain focused on what he was trying to do. As he traveled with John all across California to races, he became more competitive. Although he finished his first year of racing without a win, in his second season Jeff Gordon saw the checkered flag signaling his first victory. A victory for Jeff Gordon soon became the expected outcome of every race he entered.

As Jeff's skills improved, John began taking him to quarter-midget races all over the country, competing virtually every weekend. As the competition improved, so did Jeff. John spent more and more time tinkering with Jeff's car to make it go faster and take advantage of his increasing skill. He bought Jeff several different cars and adapted them to different track conditions.

Spectators soon became accustomed to seeing the smallest driver in the field charging to the front. Jeff was fearless and drove aggressively, a tactic that earned him more than his share of black flags, a penalty given to a driver when he breaks the rules. When a driver is black-flagged, he must pull off the track and serve a penalty, sitting out a certain number of laps. In one race, Jeff was so eager to pass another car that he actually ran right over the tire of the driver's car while passing him! Jeff was black-flagged and had to watch the next few laps from the sideline.

In the summer of 1977, Jeff collected his first major championship, the Western States. The following year, he began to dominate the quarter-midget schedule, winning a remarkable 35 races, qualifying with the fastest time in every race in which he competed, and setting numerous track records.

In the world of quarter midgets, Jeff Gordon was a superstar. The other racers called John the "Roger Penske of quarter midgets" in reference to racing-team owner Roger Penske, whose cars were dominating NASCAR competition. John began to branch out, sometimes sponsoring other drivers in cars he built. Other racers began to get jealous and whispered that John was building cars that broke the rules.

He wasn't, though. To prove it, he began selling some of Jeff's cars to other racers.

The other racers soon learned that the difference wasn't in the cars Jeff drove, but the way he drove them. They'd finish far back in the pack with the exact same car Jeff Gordon had won a race with the week before. The money John made by selling the cars helped offset the cost of taking Jeff to the races and allowed him to continue to build newer, better cars for Jeff to race in.

Over the next few years Jeff continued to dominate the quarter-midget circuit. Every weekend and during school vacations John and Jeff traveled the country to various races. Although his mother and sister joined them as often as possible, sometimes Jeff even flew back from races by himself in order not to miss school, while John drove back with Jeff's car in a trailer.

At age eight Jeff won the quarter-midget national championship. His victories were now almost automatic.

John and Carol were beginning to realize they had a prodigy on their hands. All Jeff cared about was racing. Although he did well in school, he didn't seem to mind the fact that he wasn't doing what a lot of others kids his age were doing, like playing Little League. Jeff already knew what he wanted to do with his life. He wanted to be a race-car driver.

John and Carol knew they had to continue to provide challenges for Jeff so he wouldn't become bored with the sport. Quarter-midget racing simply didn't provide Jeff with much competition anymore, and they began to tire of the way Jeff was being treated by others who were jealous of his success.

So after Jeff won the quarter-midget national championship, John and Carol decided to allow him to race go-carts, as well. Their 10-horsepower engines were more powerful than the engines used in quarter-midget racing, and the cars went much faster. The other racers were also much older than Jeff and more experienced than many of the drivers in quarter midgets. Most of the other racers were teenagers six or seven years older than Jeff. As Jeff later told a reporter, "The tracks were bigger and the speeds a lot higher. I really had to work hard."

But once Jeff saw the green flag signaling the start of a race, those differences didn't seem to affect the end result. He entered and won his first 25 go-cart races. Winning every weekend became routine.

The other go-cart drivers and their parents soon began to show the same jealousy the quarter-midget drivers had. Jeff was so much better than everyone else that the competition began to spread rumors. They said Jeff's parents had lied about his age and that he was actually much older but small enough to pass for a young boy. They thought the young racing prodigy was a fraud. With each race he won, the whispers grew louder.

It became virtually impossible for Jeff to find any competition in California in either quarter midgets or go-carts. When he won a second quarter-midget national championship in 1981 at age ten, Jeff's parents knew that it was time for Jeff to move up to another level of racing.

He began racing cars known as superstock lights. He continued to dominate, regularly beating other drivers who were as old as eighteen.

At every level in which he was competing, Jeff faced resistance from other drivers. Sometimes, his entry in a race caused other drivers to withdraw. They didn't want to have to race against him.

Jeff's stepfather sensed that his progress as a driver was beginning to stagnate. There was nothing left for him to learn in the races he was running. Jeff drove a much cleaner line around the track than most of the other drivers, meaning he didn't weave all over the track. Instead, after finding the quickest way around he followed that line over and over. He knew exactly what his car could do, and he slowly learned how to race strategically, taking advantage of both his car and his skills as a driver. He became an expert at drafting and passing other cars. He knew when to take advantage of yellow flags (when all cars have to slow down after an accident and are not allowed to pass) and when to make pit stops for fuel. To keep learning, he needed to drive longer races in faster cars.

The next level of racing was the sprint-car division. Sprint cars are both powerful and incredibly fast, going from 0–60 miles per hour in only three seconds. Their 650-horsepower engines power the small, open cars to speeds approaching 140 miles per hour. They are designed for adult drivers, and most drivers who later become professional racers begin their serious training as drivers in the sprint-car division. Sprint-car racing is considered the final step in a driver's education. In a way, the division serves the same role in NASCAR racing as minor league baseball does to the major leagues.

But as good as Jeff was, racing quarter midgets and go-carts was the relative equivalent of playing Little League and high school baseball. Moving up to race sprint cars would be a significant challenge, but Jeff and his family thought he had the ability to succeed.

Despite Jeff's obvious talent as a driver, there was just one problem. In California and in most other places in the country sprint-car racing was restricted to those old enough to have a valid driver's license.

Jeff was just beginning junior high school! He wasn't legally allowed to drive to the corner grocery store, much less to race sprint cars.

That didn't stop him, though. Jeff's stepfather approached an acquaintance, Lee Osbourne, who built and raced sprint cars, and asked him to build one. Osbourne asked John, "Don't you think you're a little old to start racing one of those cars?"

When John replied, "It's for Jeff," Osbourne was dumbfounded. At first, he didn't want to build the car for such a young driver. If Jeff had a serious accident, Osbourne knew he'd feel responsible. But when he watched Jeff race his go-cart, he realized Jeff was something special.

Even though Jeff had a car, there were still few places where he was allowed to race. At first, John took Jeff up into the California mountains. There Jeff tested his skills on lonely mountain roads or abandoned logging roads that got little traffic.

John and Jeff did manage to find a few races that allowed Jeff to compete. In February of 1984 they drove all the way across the country to Jacksonville, Florida, so Jeff could participate in the all-star Speedweek, which included one race without a minimum age requirement. But when they arrived at the track, officials tried to talk them out of racing. They never imagined that a twelve-year-old would show up to race. They thought it was too dangerous for him.

But John and Jeff refused to back down. They argued that they'd followed all the rules and had just driven all the way across the country to race. At last, the race officials gave in.

Many of the other drivers disagreed with the decision, and let John and Jeff know they weren't welcome at the track. Many looked forward to watching Jeff fail.

In his first race, he sat nervously on the track, lined up with the other drivers. As a soft rain fell, he waited for the green light that would signal the start of the race. Dressed in his fireproof racing suit and wearing a helmet and gloves, Jeff looked like a kid dressed up as a racing driver on Halloween compared to the adults in the other cars.

As the engine of his car rumbled, Jeff took a few deep breaths. He had never been so nervous in all his life.

Suddenly the cars on the track thundered to life in

an ear-shattering roar. The other cars leaped forward as Jeff, surprised by the speed of the start, struggled to get his car in gear.

He lurched from a stop and shot across the track.

There was only one problem. Jeff was supposed to be driving down the track. Instead, a combination of his nerves, the wet pavement, and being overanxious sent him out of control. The wall of the racing track loomed before him.

Fortunately, Jeff realized his mistake and was able to make a correction before crashing headlong into the wall. Still, he grazed it with his tires before cautiously maneuvering through traffic.

He couldn't believe the speed of the other cars! To Jeff, it felt as if the car was driving him instead of the other way around. Other cars seemed to be rocketing past him every few seconds and the entire race became a blur. Jeff was in over his head — and he knew it, admitting later, "I was scared to death."

Fortunately, the rain began to fall harder and after only a few laps the race was stopped and eventually canceled. The cancellation gave Jeff time to regroup. A week later, he started another race with no age restriction in Tampa, Florida.

This time, Jeff was prepared. Although he raced cautiously and fell far back of the field, he was in control. With each lap he became a little more comfortable and learned a little bit more. And in every new race he entered, he did a little better than before.

Jeff didn't dominate like he did in quarter midgets and go-carts, but by the end of the brief racing season he was creeping up in the standings.

Then he had to return to California to go back to school. But after racing sprint cars, racing quarter midgets and go-carts wasn't very exciting anymore.

For the first time in his life, Jeff began to get bored with racing.

Chapter Three:
1984-1990

Sprinting Ahead

Jeff's mother and stepfather wanted to keep him interested in racing. They knew that unless he was challenged, he might lose his desire to compete. John eased back on Jeff's schedule. Racing every weekend had become routine, so now he raced only once or twice a month. At the same time, they tried to provide him with another challenge.

John bought a boat and decided to teach Jeff how to water-ski. Jeff loved the challenge of learning a new skill. In fact, the very first time John took him waterskiing, Jeff talked his stepfather into allowing him to try skiing on just a single ski!

John showed Jeff how to hold the tow bar and how to insert his feet into the single ski. Jeff floated in the water behind the boat as John started the boat and slowly began to pull away.

As the boat accelerated, John turned around to see how Jeff was doing. He fully expected to see Jeff start to rise, then lose his balance and fall splashing into the water.

But Jeff proved just as precocious on the water as he was on the racetrack. John was shocked when he saw Jeff skimming smoothly across the surface of the water performing simple maneuvers. He was able to ski the first time he ever tried!

Jeff approached waterskiing with the same focus, determination, and drive that he demonstrated at the racetrack. Once he decided to commit himself to the sport, he wanted to be the very best. His years of driving had honed his hand-eye coordination, and after racing he wasn't afraid of going fast on the water. He soon began taking lessons and learned all sorts of special tricks, like spinning around backward and doing flips. His instructors wanted him to turn pro.

In the meantime, Jeff continued racing once or twice a month on the California go-cart and quarter-midget circuits and practicing in his sprint car. In the winter of 1986, Jeff competed in his second season of sprint racing in Florida. Although he again failed to win a race, he was very competitive, occasionally leading a race and finishing in the top five. Moreover, the other drivers began to give him some respect, offering advice and encouragement. But when the season was over, it was back to the less challenging races in California.

Jeff and his family now faced a tough decision. In order to continue his racing career, he had to find a way to race more in the sprint-car division. Or he could forget about racing all together and continue to pursue waterskiing.

Jeff enjoyed waterskiing, but he absolutely loved racing. Then John learned of a region in the country that regularly allowed drivers as young as Jeff to compete in sprint-car races.

The state of Indiana is a hotbed of automobile racing. The most famous car race in the world, the Indianapolis 500, is held there every year over the Memorial Day weekend and draws nearly half a million spectators. Due to the influence of the race, auto racing of all kinds is incredibly popular in Indiana. Small tracks of every configuration, for every type of racing, are scattered throughout the state. Sprint-car races are held for much of the year.

John learned that in Indiana the all-star series of sprint-car racing didn't have a minimum age requirement for drivers. Neither did similar races in the neighboring states of Ohio and Michigan. As long as Jeff had parental permission, he would be allowed to race. That wasn't because organizers were trying to encourage young drivers, however. They thought the rule requiring parental permission would be enough to dissuade young drivers from even thinking of competing. As Jeff later recalled, race organizers believed that "nobody was fool enough to drive [sprint cars] that young." They would soon learn otherwise.

Sprint-car racing demanded a much greater commitment than racing quarter midgets or go-carts. Sprint cars cost upwards of $25,000 to build and were expensive to maintain. It also cost a small fortune to travel from California just to compete in a race. Jeff occasionally traveled by airplane so he wouldn't miss too much school, but John still had to drive his car back and forth more than halfway across the country.

That spring Jeff competed in a small race held at the KC Speedway in Chillicothe, Ohio.

At first, it was like most of the other sprint-car races he'd competed in. He'd done well during qualifiers and had earned a coveted spot near the front at the start. Then the race started, and Jeff stayed with the front pack, jockeying for position, taking the lead only to lose it again.

That's what usually happened. As the race continued, Jeff would stay close, but he couldn't manage to regain the lead. But this race was different.

After taking the lead Jeff kept charging and held off several other drivers who were trying to pass him. This time, they couldn't. His experience matched the mechanical advantage of his car and Jeff took command.

Time and time again he whirled around the track ahead of the field. Then, he finally saw what he'd been looking for — the checkered flag.

As the race official waved the flag back and forth signaling the end of the race, Jeff roared across the finish line several car lengths ahead of the next car. At age fourteen, he had won his first sprint-car race! Now he knew that not only could he compete at the next level of racing, he could win.

The victory forced Jeff and his family to make a

difficult decision. Factoring in the length of the racing season and time they spent traveling, they quickly realized that it would be impossible for Jeff to race in the Midwest and continue to live in California. After all, he still had to attend school and do all the other things a typical teenager liked to do. It wasn't fair to expect a fourteen-year-old to spend all his extra time traveling.

So early in 1986 Jeff and his family made the hard decision to move to Indiana to give Jeff the opportunity to continue racing. But they all couldn't make the move immediately.

Jeff and his stepfather moved first, while Jeff's mother and sister stayed behind to sell the house, and so Kim could finish the school year. Jeff and his stepfather settled in Pittsboro, Indiana, a small city about twenty miles from the Indianapolis Motor Speedway. Carol and Kim joined them a few months later.

Their new life required a tremendous sacrifice. Money was tight. John gave up his business interests in California and turned his full attention to supporting Jeff's career, sometimes trading his mechanical skills for parts and tires he needed for Jeff's car.

Some drivers have the mistaken belief that Jeff Gordon was raised by a wealthy family who could afford to spend thousands of dollars supporting his career. While the Bickfords certainly did all they could to help him, they were hardly living in the lap of luxury. Even though Jeff was winning small sums racing, that money didn't begin to offset the price of maintaining a car. When they traveled to races across the Midwest, they slept in pickup trucks. There wasn't enough money to sleep in a motel.

In one way, Jeff was living a double life. On the weekends, he was a professional race-car driver, albeit at one of the lowest levels of racing. But during the week, he was just another student at Tri-West High School.

As much as possible, Jeff was just like most other teenagers. He played the saxophone (his uncle had once performed in Elvis Presley's backup band), ran cross-country, went on dates, played video games, learned to skateboard, and hung out at the mall with his friends. Like his stepfather, he also enjoyed tinkering with cars, and spent hours in the garage slowly rebuilding an old truck.

Jeff was a good student, and often tried to turn his

school projects into something involving racing. He wrote reports about racing for English and did science projects about automobile engines. He was a popular student, and everyone at Tri-West knew that all Jeff wanted to be was a race-car driver. School officials looked the other way when he called in sick to school on Fridays so he could travel to another weekend race.

Even though sprint-car racing is one of the lowest rungs of automobile racing's ladder, it is still highly competitive. Sanctioned by the United States Automobile Club (USAC), races are primarily held on small oval tracks. Some tracks are paved, but others are compacted earth known as dirt tracks. And sprint cars vary widely. Some races are held for winged cars, which have a small wing on the back that helps hold the car down on the track at high speed. Other races are for non-winged cars, which require a different set of driving skills.

The wide variety of racing conditions provided the ideal environment for Jeff to learn the ins and outs of racing. Although drivers tended to be younger men under age forty, some had been racing sprint cars for decades. The younger drivers hoped to do well and move up to other levels of racing. The competition was cutthroat, and the learning curve for a young driver like Jeff was steep.

But Jeff soaked up racing like a sponge. Using the Bloomington Speedway in nearby Bloomington, Indiana, as his home track and base of operations, Jeff improved rapidly. Nearly every time he took to the track, he posted faster and faster times. At first, his improvement showed up during pre-race qualifiers, where Jeff soon became the odds-on favorite to post the fastest time and win the coveted pole position, starting in front of the rest of the pack. Before long Jeff began to demonstrate the same speed during the races.

After winning a few races on the familiar surface of the Bloomington Speedway, Jeff began to enjoy similar success at other raceways. Ironically, just as Jeff was beginning to win on the sprint-car circuit, at Tri-West High School he was taking driver's education courses to get his driver's license!

The following year, his performance got the attention of an Australian racing enthusiast, John Rae. In 1988 Rae became Jeff's sponsor.

Sponsors are important in professional racing.

Few drivers have the money needed to finance their own careers. Sponsors help out financially in exchange for advertising and a percentage of the driver's winnings.

Sprint racing required a financial commitment beyond the means of Jeff and his family, so having a sponsor made it much easier for Jeff. Rae helped pay his expenses, both for living and for the building and maintenance of his car. He sent Jeff to Australia and New Zealand to race. Freed of financial worry, in 1988 Jeff dominated races in both places. In fifteen starts he won a remarkable fourteen times, setting a new track record in each victory!

When Jeff returned to the United States, he was no longer a young driver with great potential; he was a great driver, period. Now sixteen years old, he was allowed to join the USAC. USAC-sanctioned races were the equivalent of the major leagues of sprint cars.

In the spring of 1989, as Jeff was completing his senior year of high school, he began a remarkable run in the USAC sprint-car racing series. After winning his first USAC race in Kentucky in late May, Jeff followed with a string of strong performances.

He was so dedicated to racing that after attending graduation ceremonies at Tri-West, Jeff left immediately to compete in a race later that evening.

In many racing circuits, drivers accumulate points depending on their finish in each race. At the end of the racing season, the driver with the most points is declared the season champion. By midsummer Jeff was leading the USAC sprint-car series, with four victories.

But Jeff abruptly dropped out of the season. He didn't care about winning the sprint championship. He was focused on becoming the best driver he could possibly be, and he knew that required continuing to learn and grow as a driver. To accomplish this, he began to race in midgets, undersized Indianapolis-style open-wheel racers.

Although some consider midgets a step down from sprint-car racing, Gordon didn't look at it that way. He felt he'd shown he could race sprint cars, and wanted to demonstrate that he could be just as successful racing an entirely different kind of car. Besides, after midgets, the next level of racing was Indianapolis cars. If he ever hoped to race Indy cars, he had to prove himself in midgets.

Gordon did more than that. In his first USAC midget race he took first place and set a track record. Racing as often as twice a week, Jeff began to dominate the midget series just as he had the sprint cars.

Now that he didn't have to go to school, he could turn his full attention to racing. Jeff never gave much consideration to attending college. His racing career was progressing quickly, and he knew he couldn't take time off for college now. If he failed at racing, he could always go to college later. Jeff was named the 1989 USAC Midget Rookie of the Year.

In the 1990 season he entered 21 midget races, winning nine times to capture the midget-class championship with ease. At age nineteen, he was the youngest national champion ever.

In the racing world, Jeff was earning a name for himself. He was also reaching a time when he had to make a decision.

In the sport of automobile racing, there are three different world-class racing divisions. In Formula One, or Grand Prix racing, drivers compete in long races on street courses in fast, light, powerful, open-cockpit, open-wheeled cars known as Formula One racers. Formula One racers have wings in both the front and the back to keep them on the racecourse. The most expensive form of racing, Formula One features cars that are fast, dependable, and maneuverable. In a given race, cars might go as fast as 200 miles per hour on straightaways and as slow as 30 miles per hour as they snake through turns. One race, Le Mans, is a twenty-four-hour endurance race. But Grand Prix racing is more popular elsewhere in the world than in the United States. It wasn't attractive to Jeff.

Indy cars are similar to Formula One cars in that they, too, are light and have open cockpits and open wheels. But Indy cars, aerodynamically shaped like a bullet, are designed to race primarily on closed tracks. Although they reach speeds of more than 240 miles per hour, they aren't as maneuverable as Formula One cars. But due primarily to the popularity of the Indianapolis 500, Indy-car racing is much more popular in the United States than Formula One racing.

The other division is stock car, or NASCAR racing. NASCAR stands for National Association for Stock Car Auto Racing. NASCAR is the most popular form of auto racing in the United States, and developed from races first held between stock car models made by American automobile manufacturers. Even now, stock cars look a lot like standard automobiles, but they have much more powerful engines. Stock cars, which are much heavier than either Formula One or Indy cars, usually race on oval tracks for distances of between 200 and 600 miles. They, too, go well over 200 miles per hour.

Jeff knew that the time was soon approaching when he would have to decide which direction he would take his racing career. He didn't want to race midget or sprint cars forever, and he was quickly running out of competition at those levels.

Would he race Indy cars or stock cars? That decision would prove to be the most important of his young life.

Chapter Four:

1990-1991

Going to School

Even as he continued to race — and dominate — in both the sprint-car and midget divisions of USAC, Gordon and his parents discussed his future. Indy-car racing, because of the influence of the nearby Indianapolis Motor Speedway, site of the Indy 500, was attractive to him. Midget cars resemble scaled-down Indy cars, and in interviews following midget wins, Gordon often spoke of his desire to someday race an Indy car.

But Indy-car racing is extremely expensive and extremely dangerous. Great strides have been made in making the cars safe, but the open cockpit is inherently dangerous, particularly if a car rolls during an accident. Although a roll bar, which during an accident allows the car to roll over the cockpit, and other safety devices provide the driver with some protection, severe injuries and occasional deaths are not unknown in Indy racing. Gordon's parents had faith in their son's skills, but they still worried about his safety. In addition, there was some resistance in Indy racing to drivers as young as Gordon. He would need a sponsor, but no one was willing to risk the great expense to maintain an Indy car on a driver so young.

Gordon's parents guided him toward stock-car racing, which they considered safer and which offered different levels of racing for drivers with different levels of skill and experience. Sponsorship was also easier to come by, as companies paid drivers to put stickers advertising their products on the sides of their cars. Yet even after Gordon won the USAC sprint-car dirt-track championship in 1991, he was still considered too young and too inexperienced — despite more than 500 wins in his career — to move directly into NASCAR racing.

But there was a place he could learn. In North Carolina, NASCAR Hall of Fame driver Buck Baker operated a school where he taught young drivers the ins and outs of NASCAR racing. At his parents' urging, Gordon agreed to attend Baker's school.

Gordon's mother traveled with him to North Carolina. The television network ESPN was intrigued by Gordon's story and decided to cover his experience at the school. Baker allowed him to attend for free in exchange for the publicity he brought.

When Gordon first climbed into one of Baker's stock cars, it was an alien experience. The stock car weighed three times more than either a sprint or midget car and was much, much larger. Then Gordon flipped the switch that electronically starts the car and began to drive.

He loved the surge of power he felt behind the wheel of the car. Within moments, he knew that he was meant to drive stock cars. As he later told a reporter, "I said to myself, 'This is it. This is what I want to do.' It [the car] felt big and heavy, but very fast. I knew right away that stock-car racing was the way I wanted to go."

Gordon's driving talent was obvious as he adapted quickly to the larger, more powerful car. The nuances of stock-car racing, such as drafting, or racing close to the car ahead to cut down wind resistance and save fuel, then passing by swinging down below the car and slingshotting past, came as second nature to Gordon.

He was even able to convince his mother to ride along with him. Before they started, she cautioned her son not to drive too fast.

Jeff started the car and slowly pulled from the pits, then accelerated quickly as he shifted the car into gear and pulled onto the track. By the time he reached the first, high-banked turn, he was going in excess of 100 miles per hour. Had he been going any slower, the car would have slipped down the 30-degree embankment.

As Gordon later told a reporter, his mother started to panic and screamed, "Slow down, slow down!"

Bur Gordon continued to accelerate, the picture of calm. "Mom," he explained, "the car won't go any slower." In just the first of the car's four gears, the 700-horsepower engine powers the car to 65 miles per hour. Second gear takes it well over 100 miles per hour, and by fourth gear the car approaches 200 miles per hour. That was the last time Gordon's mother ever agreed to ride in one of his race cars.

On his second day at the school, a man named Hugh Connerly, who owned and sponsored stock cars, spotted Gordon and his obvious talent. He wanted to know if Gordon would be interested in racing in the Busch Grand National Series, a series of stock-car races that serves as the training ground for NASCAR's top series, the Winston Cup.

Gordon was thrilled. At the end of the day he couldn't wait to call his stepfather. When John answered the phone Gordon didn't even wait for him to speak.

"Sell everything!" he blurted out breathlessly, referring to his sprint and midget cars. "We're going into stock-car racing!"

John shared Gordon's excitement, but he was more cautious. Bickford knew that becoming competitive on the stock-car circuit was an expensive undertaking that cost several million dollars, and he questioned whether Connerly had both the financial resources and the commitment needed to take Gordon to the next level of racing. Even drivers with Gordon's extensive racing background often had a difficult time finding success racing in NASCAR. One simple mistake resulting in a wreck can destroy hundreds of thousands of dollars of equipment and months of work. He worried that if Gordon made a mistake, Connerly might drop him and that subsequent car owners wouldn't give Gordon another chance.

But Gordon was determined, and Connerly eagerly signed Gordon up to compete in the final three races of the 1990 Busch Series.

Getting Gordon on the track in an official race was a complicated process. He couldn't just be handed a car. Getting a car and driver on the track required the combined efforts of dozens of people.

Months before entering a race, the car owner must put together a team dedicated to building and maintaining as many as three or four cars (backups are needed in case of accidents or mechanical trouble) and manning the pits during a race. One group at the race shop, the garage crew, concentrates on the building of the car, while the pit crew focuses on maintaining and supporting the car during a race.

In the garage, skilled engineers, mechanics, and machinists build the car from the ground up according to the strict and complicated NASCAR rule book, which ensures that all cars adhere to certain standards in regard to weight, engine size and power, suspension systems, braking, etc. Although the end result resembles a standard car produced on the assembly line, over the years NASCAR automobiles have evolved into specialized machines that share little with their off-the-lot predecessors.

While many car parts can be purchased, others must be made from scratch or adapted from standard parts. At each step of the car-building process, the garage crew must ensure that the car is durable, mechanically sound, and as safe as possible. The fastest car in the world finishes last if it keeps breaking down.

Parts are tested over and over again during the building process to make sure everything is in working order. Only then is the driver allowed to take the car onto the track for an extensive period of testing.

Through a lengthy process of trial and error, the garage staff tries to tweak the car to extract as much speed as possible without sacrificing either control or safety. During these tests they make hundreds of tiny changes, ranging from switching tires and adjusting air pressure to making minute adjustments to the transmission or gearing system of the car. And each time the driver takes the track, there is the chance that he might have an accident or blow an engine. Even a momentary brush against the wall or a seemingly harmless spinout can cause extensive damage that might take days or even weeks to repair.

While the car is being tested, the pit crew also begins training. The crew usually consists of a crew chief and eight other men, each with a specific role in maintaining the car when it pulls into the pits during a race.

The gas man is responsible for filling the car with fuel, dumping a 22-gallon tank of gasoline into the car in a matter of seconds. Two other men, known as carriers, do nothing but carry new tires over the pit wall to the car, while two tire changers, one for the front of the car and one for the rear, remove the tires with an air wrench and replace them. Another member of the crew, the jack man, lifts the car with a jack, while another, the catcher, is responsible for getting the old tires off the track as fast as possible. The spotter communicates with the driver by means of a chalkboard or radio and helps schedule the pit stops.

The entire operation is managed by the crew chief, who performs a role similar to that of a football coach. Apart from the driver, the crew chief is probably more responsible for the performance of the car in the race than any other man. The crew chief is responsible for putting the crew together and overseeing practice sessions where they perform their duties hundreds of times until they do so flawlessly and as quickly as possible. He must be very organized, knowledgeable about every facet of the car, driver, track, and competition, and be able to motivate other team members and earn their respect. Moreover, he must be a great race strategist and have the complete trust of the driver. His decisions must be executed without any questions.

When a car enters the pits, timing is everything. Since every car has to pit several times during a race for more fuel and new tires, a slower car that makes quick pit stops can win a race over a faster car that spends too much time in the pit. Races are won in the pits as often as they are on the track. The best teams can refuel a car, change all four tires, and clean the windshield, which gets covered with oil and debris during a race, in less than 17 seconds. On occasion, they also make minor mechanical adjustments. Their ability to do so with the greatest possible speed is key.

In order to get Gordon on the track in the Busch Series, Connerly had to put together just such a team. He already had a garage crew in place, but he needed to recruit a pit crew.

Good crew chiefs are at a premium in racing. The best are recruited by the best drivers. To race in the Busch Series, Connerly couldn't recruit an established, top-shelf crew chief.

But just as he had picked out Gordon as a young driver with potential, he also selected a young crew chief, Ray Evernham, to run the pits. When Evernham met Gordon for the first time, the two men immediately hit it off. Even though Evernham was several years older than Gordon, they both realized that they shared the same focus, dedication, and love for racing. Gordon grew to depend on Evernham for support just as he had depended on John Bickford. Evernham, in fact, reminded Gordon of his stepfather in many ways.

After putting the team together and building and testing the car, Gordon was finally ready to race. But that didn't mean he automatically earned a place in the starting lineup of a race.

Apart from the experience of the driver, the Busch Series differs from the Winston Cup Series in several important respects. Most Busch events are only 300-mile races, while Winston races are usually 500 miles. Busch races are also held on Saturdays instead of Sundays, and the prize money is much less.

At every race, each car must qualify in order to compete. The entire team arrives at the track several days before the race to ready the car and attempt to qualify.

Qualifiers are timed practice runs that every car and driver must complete. They are held in order to keep the field of racers to a manageable size and to ensure that every car in the race is capable of going fast enough to race safely. A car that can't stay within three or four miles per hour of the fastest car on the track would be a dangerous impediment in a race. In the Busch Series as many as 43 cars can qualify and compete in a single race.

Qualifying times determine the order of the cars at the beginning of the race. In NASCAR races, cars begin the race from a running start, meaning all cars are already running around the track in orderly rows behind a pace car before the checkered flag signaling the beginning of the race is waved.

The fastest qualifier earns the pole position, the inside spot in the front row. This gives the driver a great advantage at the start, because he needn't work his way through a lot of traffic. He has a clear path ahead and is often able to bolt out to the lead.

In Gordon's first attempt to qualify for a Busch Series race, he failed. Problems with the car, coupled with his relative inexperience at driving a stock car, combined to keep him out of the race.

Gordon was disappointed, but undeterred. It would be a long, long time before Jeff Gordon would fail to qualify for a race again.

Chapter Five:

1991–1992

Heading Toward the Majors

Gordon quickly showed that he was as adaptable to NASCAR racing as he had been when he first began racing midgets and sprint cars. After a brief period of adjustment, he began to enjoy some success, steadily moving up in the finish race by race.

By the beginning of the 1991 Busch season, Gordon's period of adjustment had ended. He left Hugh Connerly and began driving for another owner, Bill Davis, taking Ray Evernham and much of his crew with him.

Close followers of racing quickly identified Gordon as an up-and-comer on the NASCAR circuit. His distinctive white Ford with the number one became familiar to racing fans who watched the Busch Series races on television.

In most races he easily made the top ten, and

although he failed to win a race, he finished second twice and third another time. It was an impressive performance for a driver who had yet to turn twenty-one years old, and was enough to earn him Rookie of the Year honors for the Busch Series.

Race fans were intrigued by Gordon, not just for the way he drove, but because of his youth and good looks. Before he even won a race, he had his own fan club.

Gordon's performance in 1991 attracted the attention of a major sponsor, the company that makes the Baby Ruth candy bar. The days of trading for car parts and sleeping in the back of a pickup truck were well over.

In 1992, Gordon and his team blossomed. With the influx of cash provided by his sponsor, combined with his own experience and determination, Gordon's car began to be a serious threat in every race he entered.

In March of 1992 at the Atlanta 300 in Atlanta, Georgia, Gordon was driving hard, trying for the lead. He was running with a car veteran observers would call "loose," meaning that it was designed to go faster in the corners but was difficult to control, sometimes skidding sideways and threatening to come off the track.

Time and time again Gordon powered into the turns while fans held their breath and wondered if he could maintain control. Time and time again he did, exhibiting a level of skill and nerve seen in only the best drivers.

One such observer was a man named Rick Hendrick. As he watched, he told a companion, "Watch this guy [Gordon]. In a lap or two he's gonna bust his fanny [crash]."

A wealthy car dealer, Hendrick had used his fortune to bankroll Hendrick Motorsports, sponsoring several cars at a time in the Winston Cup Series. At the time, most owners sponsored only a single driver.

Hendrick took a different approach. Sponsoring multiple cars and drivers allowed him to put together a much larger racing team, one that employed a total of nearly 200 people. Included on his payroll were several engineers, and the Hendrick Motorsports facility in Charlotte, North Carolina, was a state-of-the-art facility that looked more like a plant in the aerospace industry than an automobile garage. His various teams shared facilities and information, making the whole operation more efficient. The concentrated effort his company was able to put into the sport had paid off at the finish line. Several of Hendrick's drivers, like Geoff Bodine and Darrell Waltrip, were among the most successful drivers in NASCAR.

Hendrick's premonition turned out to be wrong. Like the other fans that day, he saw Gordon push his car right to the edge, yet somehow retain control. Although he didn't have the fastest car in the field that day, he nonetheless managed to keep pace with Winston Cup drivers like Dale Earnhardt, who was running in the Busch race to get used to the track for a later Winston Cup race.

The more he watched Gordon, the more impressed Hendrick became. He saw that Gordon wasn't being reckless, but knew precisely how far he could push his car and what he could get away with. As far as he was concerned, Gordon was the best driver in the race.

That may well have been true. For despite racing in thousands of races in varying conditions in all kinds of cars since he was five years old, Jeff Gordon had never, ever had a bad accident on the racetrack.

He knew what he was doing, and on that day he went on to win the race even against drivers like Earnhardt.

Gordon won two additional races and set a record by winning the pole position in eleven races. People were starting to talk about him as the next big thing in racing, and most expected owner Bill Davis to move Gordon up to compete in the Winston Cup races in 1992.

But Davis was still lining up the additional sponsors he would need to move up to the Winston Cup. He was courting the Ford automobile company, a big-time sponsor that would be able to spend the millions of dollars required to be competitive. But in the meantime, he didn't have Gordon under contract.

When Hendrick found that out, he knew what he wanted to do. He had an opening on his team for a driver and he wanted that driver to be Jeff Gordon. He had met Gordon on several occasions and had been just as impressed by Gordon's soft-spoken demeanor and clean-cut image as he was by his skills behind the wheel of a car. Hendrick was smart enough to know that racing would be more and more expensive each year and that sponsors would become an even more important part of the racing scene. And as he told one observer, Jeff Gordon "was a sponsor's dream." He asked him to join his team.

But Hendrick wasn't the only other owner interested in Gordon. Legendary driver Cale Yarborough also had a team and approached Gordon about joining him in the Winston Cup in 1993. Gordon and his stepfather, who still served as a valuable advisor to Gordon, entertained Yarborough's offer seriously. But they wanted to bring Ray Evernham and their own pit crew along, an idea Yarborough dismissed, for he already employed his own crews. So they began to consider Rick Hendrick's offer.

Gordon didn't really want to leave Bill Davis. But he'd grown impatient waiting for Davis to line up his Ford sponsorship, and Ford didn't seem in a hurry to sign on. In addition, he was impressed with Hendrick's more professional approach to racing.

Yet at the same time, switching teams was risky. If he stayed with Davis, Gordon knew he would be the focus of the attention of the entire team. With Hendrick, he would be only one of three drivers, and as the youngest and least experienced in NASCAR racing, he worried that he might not receive the same level of support as the other drivers.

But Hendrick wanted Gordon badly. He told him he could bring along Ray Evernham and his crew. Gordon knew that with Hendrick's connections, acquiring a major sponsor would prove to be no problem.

After weighing his options, Gordon decided to go with Hendrick. He signed a standard driver's contract that guaranteed him a salary. Any prize money he won would be split with Hendrick Motorsports.

His decision was controversial in the NASCAR world. Hendrick's multi-team approach to racing was relatively new, and many veteran drivers and owners didn't think it was fair. Gordon was also criticized for leaving Bill Davis, toward whom many thought Gordon had been ungracious. Moreover, Gordon had been driving a Ford for Davis, but would drive a Chevrolet for Hendrick, a switch that angered Ford devotees.

But Gordon was accustomed to criticism. Other drivers had been jealous of him ever since he started racing. Besides, he felt that Davis and Ford had had ample opportunity to sign him to a contract. Had they moved more quickly, he would have been happy to stay. Their hesitation made him question their commitment to him. Hendrick Motorsports, on the other hand, made it clear they wanted Gordon and that they had the means to help him succeed.

With his contract status resolved, Gordon looked forward to focusing on the only thing he really cared about — racing. He was ready for the Winston Cup Series, and the Winston Cup Series was ready for him.

Chapter Six:
1993–1994

Rookie of the Year

Stock-car racing has a long and colorful history. It starts with Prohibition.

In the 1920s, the manufacture and sale of alcohol were prohibited in the United States. Even so, bootleggers made whiskey and other spirits deep in the Appalachian mountains, carrying on a tradition that had existed for decades.

But now that tradition was illegal. Government tax officials, known as revenue agents, scoured the countryside looking for illegal stills and the men who transported the product in bulk to larger cities.

These smugglers usually transported whiskey in souped-up-jalopies — old cars with powerful engines that could outrace the revenue agents and sheriffs in a chase.

The smugglers often got together to swap stories

and compare their cars. One would boast that his car was faster than the others. Before too long an impromptu, and often illegal, race was underway.

After Prohibition ended, some of these drivers continued to race on small tracks throughout the south. In 1947, a man named Bill France created NASCAR, the National Association for Stock Car Auto Racing. Under his stewardship, NASCAR grew from a loosely organized group that often raced on horse tracks to a professional organization with modern racetracks throughout the country.

As television became more popular in the 1960s, NASCAR racing began to find a national audience. In 1971, the Winston cigarette brand became NASCAR's major sponsor. Throughout the 1970s and 1980s, NASCAR grew rapidly as cable television networks, like ESPN, broadcast the sport on a regular basis. Drivers like Richard Petty and Junior Johnson became wealthy driving on the NASCAR circuit.

Yet many observers still saw NASCAR as a bunch of guys from the backwoods racing hot rods. Some didn't take it as a serious sport. They thought that its appeal was based on the fact that fans liked to see car crashes, but didn't really care who won or how good the racing was. They believed the sport's fan base would always be limited to a small but rabid group centered in the South.

More visionary NASCAR fans believed that all their sport needed to become as big as pro football or baseball was a new generation of drivers, fresh faces that younger fans all over America could identify with. They thought NASCAR was a sleeping giant.

Jeff Gordon came to NASCAR at the perfect time. The sport needed a driver like Gordon, and Gordon — young, good-looking, modest, and artic-ulate — soon proved to be the perfect symbol to lead NASCAR into a new era.

Soon after joining Hendrick Motorsports, Gordon returned to the track. That fall Hendrick entered him in his first Winston Cup race, the Hooters 500 in Atlanta, Georgia, the final race of the season. Only twenty-one years old, Gordon was now racing in the major leagues.

His first challenge was to qualify for the race, no easy feat for a Winston Cup rookie. After all, the other drivers in the race were veterans who had either been successful for a long time or had proven themselves in the Busch Series.

But Gordon was ready. In a practice run he blistered the track by setting a new record of more than 181 miles per hour. For a rookie, that was unheard of.

Yet when he took the track later to make an official qualifying run, his nerves showed. After breaking the track record he qualified fully three miles per hour slower, in 21st place. That was okay, for it was solidly in the middle of the pack, ahead of many veterans. For a driver to qualify for a Winston Cup race in his first attempt was rare.

Then the race began. Although Gordon ran well, his car simply wasn't up to par with others in the race. Gordon didn't have quite enough experience driving the car to know what it could do. After staying close to the lead pack for much of the race, he cut a tire and fell back to finish in 31st place, winning just more than $6,000.

But having him compete in a Winston Cup race in 1992 had been a strategic decision by Hendrick. He wanted Gordon to get his feet wet so that when the

1993 season started, he'd already have a race under his belt.

In the off-season, they turned their attention to building a car specifically for Gordon. All winter long they built and tested the car.

This was a luxury Gordon had never had before. In the past, he'd often found that he'd had to adapt to the car he was driving. But Hendrick built a car to match his driving style.

Gordon's team wasn't satisfied until the car was perfect. During test runs, when Gordon complained about the handling or the gear ratio, they thought nothing of taking the car back into the garage, taking it apart, and trying to get it right.

When the car was finally unveiled in the spring, it was an eye-catcher.

The Chevy was unlike any other car in NASCAR, most of which are a single color. But Gordon's number 24 sported a rainbow across the hood, which dissolved into a wide blue stripe before transforming into another rainbow pattern on the rear of the car. The design led Gordon's pit crew to call themselves the Rainbow Warriors.

Some observers looked at the car and laughed.

They thought it was too showy for an unproven rookie. But Gordon's car was distinctive. His team knew that fans would be able to spot it anywhere on the track. They wanted Gordon to stand out from the field from his first race on.

The first race of the NASCAR season is also the biggest race of the year, the Daytona 500.

The Daytona 500 has a long and storied history. The beach at Daytona is wide and flat, and men began racing automobiles on the beach more than one hundred years ago. When Bill France started NASCAR, some of the first races were held on the sands of Daytona.

But racing on sand, while exciting, also limits the speed of the cars and the number of fans who can attend. Although some races were held on dirt tracks and on small paved tracks, France wanted to preserve racing at Daytona and build the ultimate stock-car track. He had in mind a much larger facility with huge grandstands.

But in order to attract a big crowd, France knew he had to have more than just a long track. It also had to be fast.

He satisfied both requirements in 1959, when he

built the first modern NASCAR track in Daytona. An enormous, banked oval two and a half miles in length, the track was designed so fans could see the entire track from the grandstand, with steep turns and long straightaways that guaranteed that drivers would be able to maintain their speed all around the track.

As veteran driver Lee Petty (father of driver Richard Petty) said when the track first opened, "We knew that stock-car racing was never going to be the same again." Fans loved the track. The big crowds led to a huge purse that made the Daytona 500 NASCAR's signature race, just as the Indianapolis 500 is the premier Indy-car race and Le Mans the foremost Formula One race. If a NASCAR driver could win only one race, most would choose the Daytona 500.

The 1993 race was even more important, for it would be the first NASCAR race in years without driver Richard Petty. Petty, the most successful driver in NASCAR history, had retired. In a career that started in 1958, he had won the driving title a record seven times, winning a remarkable 200 races. His retirement marked the end of an era.

Few suspected it at the time, but a new era was ready to begin. Jeff Gordon was about to make his mark.

As the first race of the season, qualifying is done differently at Daytona. Although the pole position still goes to the driver with the fastest two-lap time, all others must qualify in one of two 125-mile qualifying races.

During practice runs, Gordon had impressed veteran driver Dale Earnhardt. Earnhardt helped him learn the track during practice, driving as if it were a real race so Gordon could practice passing and drafting. Earnhardt wasn't just being nice. Rookie drivers are often the cause of accidents. In their first season, they must drive with a stripe painted on the backs of their cars to warn other drivers that they are inexperienced. Neither Earnhardt nor any other driver wants to get into an accident, so helping Gordon out was just common sense. It made the race safer for everyone.

In Gordon's qualifier, he bolted out front and demonstrated a savvy beyond his years in the 50-lap race. He held off all challengers and became the first rookie in thirty years to win a qualifier, and the youngest winner ever. Gordon earned a lot of fans that day. Some spectators had rented race scanners, which allowed them to listen in on the radio communication between the driver and the pit. They could hear the excitement and wonder in Gordon's voice. As he told the press later, "If you were on the radio, you would have heard a whole lot of screaming excitement!"

Gordon was so shocked by his win that after the checkered flag, he circled the track one extra time, looking for the victory lane. He didn't know where it was on the track!

"Never been there," he quipped to the press later. But he soon proved he knew his way around the racetrack. At the ceremony where he received his trophy, he couldn't help but notice one of the presenters, "Winston Girl" Brooke Sealey. Soon afterward, he asked her out on a date. A year later she became Mrs. Jeff Gordon.

His performance marked him as a driver to watch in the 500, although no one gave him a serious chance to win. After all, in the qualifying race, many veterans hold back a little to save their cars and their energy for the race that really matters.

But no one told Gordon that. Starting from the inside position on the second row, he showed he was out to win. As the flag waved marking the start of the race, Gordon bolted to the lead, becoming the first rookie ever to lead the first lap.

Although he couldn't hold the lead, he stayed close. Each time the leader rocketed past the grandstand, there was the rainbow-colored car, just a split second behind. With three laps remaining, Gordon still clung to second place behind Dale Earnhardt.

Yet there were other contenders grouped behind Gordon. With only three laps to go, each driver prepared to make his move.

One lap later, Dale Jarrett, running third, managed to nose past Gordon and take over second place.

Gordon had to make a decision. To keep pace as the cars entered the next turn, he had to draft behind either Earnhardt or Jarrett. If he chose correctly, he would be able to draft behind the leader, take back second place, and have a chance to go for the lead on the final lap. But if he guessed wrong, he'd fall farther back. With only a fraction of a second to decide, he chose to stay with Earnhardt.

Just as he did, Jarrett shot ahead, bringing the car behind him, driven by Geoff Bodine, along. In just a few seconds Gordon had fallen to fourth place.

Try as he might, over the remaining two laps he just couldn't catch up. As he continued to jockey for position, the checkered flag waved, and yet another car nosed ahead of him to steal fourth place. Gordon finished fifth, earning $110,000.

He was disappointed, but also thrilled. To finish fifth in his first Daytona 500 was a remarkable accomplishment. Almost overnight Jeff Gordon went from being "Jeff Who?" to becoming one of the hottest names in racing. Crew chief Ray Evernham spoke for the entire team when he said after the race, "I don't think anybody really knows just how talented Jeff Gordon is. Even he doesn't know."

Everyone would soon find out.

Chapter Seven:
1994–1995

Down Victory Lane

Everyone began to expect big things from Jeff Gordon. Fans were used to watching rookies struggle, but after Gordon's impressive debut at Daytona everyone looked for him to contend in every race. So did Gordon. At every level he'd raced in thus far, once he'd cracked the top five, a string of victories had soon followed.

But some funny things happened on the way to the finish line. Actually, they weren't funny at all. They were rather typical mistakes for rookie drivers to make on the Winston Cup circuit.

In his second race, the Goodwrench 500, Gordon qualified far back in the pack, then blew an engine early in the race to finish a disappointing 34th. He rebounded in his next race to finish sixth, then was the fourth qualifier at the Motorcraft 400.

He led for much of the race and for a time it appeared as if he was on his way to his first Winston Cup win. But Gordon made a critical, rookie mistake.

Early in the race, he drove his car too hard, using fuel much too rapidly. Although he was leading the race with only twelve laps remaining, he was forced to make a quick pit stop to take on more fuel.

Despite the fact that his pit crew performed their roles to perfection and had him in and out of the pits in a matter of seconds, Gordon's miscalculation cost him. Three cars passed him while he was in the pits. They had raced more conservatively and didn't need to make an extra stop for fuel. Gordon finished a disappointing fourth, but he learned a valuable lesson about fuel management.

Much of the rest of the season followed a similar pattern. One or two or three good races and high finishes in a row would be followed by a similar string of disappointing runs marred by small mistakes, minor accidents, and mechanical trouble. In one race, the Coca-Cola 600, Gordon was leading when he accelerated too quickly during a restart, earning a one-lap penalty. He still finished second, but the error cost him a win.

Even so, he managed to finish in the top five in six different races, good enough for 14th place in the Winston Cup standings, a tremendous finish for a rookie. He won a total of more than $700,000 in prize money and was named Winston Cup Rookie of the Year, worth a $25,000 bonus. He summed up his performance by saying accurately, "We had a good year and I learned a lot racing against the best drivers in the world." But Jeff Gordon was a young man in a hurry. "I can't wait til next year," he added. Everyone knew that in 1994 he wouldn't be satisfied with learning. He wanted to win.

Early in the 1994 season, he achieved his goal. He won the season's inaugural event, the all-star Busch Clash at Daytona, a race that consisted of two 10-lap sprints. Unfortunately, that race didn't count in the official Winston Cup standings. Still, a win was a win, and Gordon looked ahead to the Daytona 500.

He raced well at Daytona and finished fourth. Two races later he was running strong when he reached the pits and was shocked to see his left front tire come off and start rolling away! Fortunately, his car wasn't damaged and the pit crew was able to replace the wheel. But the miscue, likely caused by pit crew error during an earlier tire change, again cost him a win. Still, an eventual victory seemed inevitable.

But over the next several months, Gordon and his team stumbled, putting together a string of disappointing finishes. Critics began to whisper that perhaps Gordon was in over his head, that the Rainbow Warriors weren't a topnotch pit crew, and that Hendrick Motorsports was overrated. Some even thought Jeff's relationship with Brooke was the cause of his trouble.

Gordon shrugged off the criticism. He knew that he was competing at the highest level of racing, where in order to win just about everything had to go perfectly. If it didn't, another driver was certain to take advantage.

In the eleventh race of the season, the Coca-Cola 600, Gordon and his crew rolled out a new race car, one Gordon dubbed "Brooker" after his wife. In qualifying he rocketed around the track to win the pole position easily, his first pole of the season.

Brimming with confidence in his new car, Gordon

jumped out ahead at the start of the grueling 600-mile contest, a race so long that it was scheduled to finish after dark.

But Gordon soon gave up the lead, a strategic decision made to save fuel. In a race of any distance, it really doesn't matter who is leading until the checkered flag.

For much of the race Gordon hung just a few car lengths behind leaders Rusty Wallace, Geoff Bodine, and Dale Jarrett, who dueled for the lead. He was sure he had enough car to stay with the leaders, but he was also learning. Being fast wasn't always enough to win a close race. Sometimes a driver has to be able to out-think the competition.

With only 30 laps remaining, every driver in the lead pack was asking himself, "Should I pit?" Each team knew that if they went to the pits too early, under a green flag, and the competition was able to wait and pit during a yellow caution flag, it could cost them the race. Timing the final pit stop was everything.

Each team waited until the last instant, when it became clear that they couldn't afford to wait for a yellow flag that might never come. Wallace came off the track first, getting four new tires and a splash of fuel. He was soon followed by Bodine. Jarrett had fallen back and Gordon was in the lead.

Then Gordon and Ray Evernham made the call that won the race. Gordon came into the pits for fuel and tires, but instead of changing all four tires, Evernham only changed the tires on the right side of the car, saving six or eight valuable seconds. When Gordon came back on the track, he was still ahead.

But it was also a risky decision. If either of the tires on his left side failed, Gordon could crash. Moreover, the team knew that by changing two tires they were sacrificing some speed and control. It was a gamble designed to keep Gordon in the lead. It would be up to him to keep it.

They needn't have worried. Gordon drove brilliantly the remainder of the race, drafting and then slingshotting past slower cars to make up for his loss of traction and speed. Incredibly, Gordon was able to increase his lead, and crossed the finish line nearly four seconds ahead of the second-place finisher. He had finally won!

In the pits, Gordon's Rainbow Warriors went

crazy, jumping up and down and hugging each other while Gordon took his victory lap with tears of joy streaming down his face. When he finally reached the winner's circle, he was so overcome he could hardly speak.

"This is the happiest day of my life," he finally blurted out. "You can't imagine how hard it is to get to this point," he added. "The pit stop won it for us. It was a great call."

But Gordon recovered by the time he was awarded the first-place check for $196,500. When he saw those numbers, he joked that they ought to just "round it up" to a cool $200,000. Standing nearby, track owner Bruton Smith saw the opportunity to get a little extra publicity and did just that. He walked over to Gordon, opened his wallet, peeled off thirty-five 100-dollar bills, and handed them to Gordon.

The breakthrough win marked the start of a string of strong performances. But Gordon couldn't wait for win number two.

The Brickyard 400 was a new NASCAR race, the first held at the famed Indianapolis Motor Speedway, site of the Indy 500 and close to Gordon's childhood home in Pittsboro. As a young boy, he had dreamed of racing at Indianapolis, but when he had decided to race stock cars, it appeared as if he'd never fulfill his dream. But, in part because of Gordon, interest in NASCAR racing was growing rapidly and the organization was able to gain access to the fabled track.

He wanted to win the race badly, calling it "a dream come true," and saying, "I don't think I ever wanted something so badly [as] to win [the first Brickyard]." All his old friends were certain to be in the crowd.

Interest in the race was intense. It sported the biggest prize money in NASCAR history and drew the largest crowd to ever witness a NASCAR race.

It was also one of NASCAR's more challenging races. The track at Indianapolis had been built for cars of another style in another era, when they were much slower. The turns weren't banked nearly as steeply as those at other racetracks, meaning that drivers would have to be extra careful to make sure they didn't wreck.

Gordon and his team even decided to switch cars for the race. They didn't want to make a whole lot of changes to Gordon's number-one car, then have to change it back for the next race. So they made the necessary adjustments to one of his backup cars.

Gordon was delighted with the way the car ran during qualifying, where he finished third. "The first lap in practice, I knew we had a great car," he said later. At the start of the race he was confident he could win.

The race got off to a rough start. Several drivers barely avoided causing accidents on the first lap as they adapted to the unfamiliar track. Then, a bit later in the race, Gordon nearly collided with several other cars that spun out of control after accidents. But that didn't prevent him from charging to the front.

With only 25 laps to go, Gordon and Ernie Irvan, one of NASCAR's best drivers, were locked in a duel for the lead. For the remainder of the race, fans were thrilled as they watched the two men trade the lead back and forth several times. But neither man was able to pull away. They rocketed down the track, one trailing the other by inches.

Then Gordon and his team made a critical decision. From the pits, Ray Evernham suggested that Gordon drop down inside Irvan and run side by side with the veteran driver. The tactic took Irvan out of his line and forced him to run on a portion of the track that wasn't as smooth as the line occupied by Gordon. They hoped that would cause Irvan's tires to wear down so that at the finish Gordon, with slightly better traction, would be able to nudge ahead.

Four laps from the end, as the two cars raced side by side, Gordon noticed Irvan's car shudder and shimmy slightly, an indication he was having trouble with his tires. Gordon slowly eased his car toward Irvan's, forcing him a little wider.

Suddenly Irvan dropped back as Gordon shot into the lead. Gordon's ploy had worked! Irvan had blown a tire!

The crowd went wild as Gordon tore around the track on the final few laps and took the checkered flag alone, four car lengths ahead of second-place finisher Brett Bodine. As he did, Gordon's life changed dramatically. Before the Brickyard, he was known as a young driver who had a chance to be great. Now, he was known as a great driver, period. The victory made Gordon a familiar name all across the country, not just to racing fans, but to sports fans with only a passing interest in racing.

Once again, tears started streaming down his face. As if he never wanted to leave the track, Gordon took *two* victory laps to get his emotions under control, telling the press later that he didn't want "to be known as a crybaby all the time." Then he pulled into the winner's circle where he was greeted by the jubilant members of his team.

To win a race at Indy was the culmination of a boyhood dream. Gordon later described the race as "bigger than life." He said with pride, "There's only gonna be one winner of the first race, and I'm that guy. This is the happiest day of my life." The winner's check for $613,000 didn't hurt, either.

Veteran drivers, the press, and fans alike sensed that they were witnessing something special. Ernie Irvan was effusive in his praise of Gordon. "He has a lot — a lot — of raw talent," he said of Gordon.

"He's already done things when most of us were not even sitting in a Winston car. I know I'll be racing him most of my career."

"The Kid," said Ray Evernham in reference to Gordon, "is phenomenal."

Chapter Eight:
1995

That Championship Season

Gordon soon learned that with his newfound celebrity status came a new set of expectations. Before the race, he'd agreed to make an appearance the next day before his old fans from Pittsboro at the nearby Tri-County Speedway. The whole town was expected to turn out to greet their favorite son.

But when Gordon won the race, NASCAR had other plans. The inaugural Brickyard race was important to the organization. They had made arrangements for the winner to go to Walt Disney World as part of their agreement with Disney, which had been a major sponsor of the race.

Gordon hated to back out of his commitment, but he knew that he owed NASCAR a significant debt and had to do whatever he could to help the organization. Predictably, some critics charged that Gordon had "gone Hollywood" and didn't care about his old friends anymore.

But most of the people in Pittsboro understood. Jeff's mother and stepfather appeared in his stead, and they played a tape of the last twenty minutes of Gordon's pit communication during the race, allowing his fans the vicarious thrill of listening in as he and Evernham plotted their victory.

The win vaulted Gordon into the top ten in the Winston Cup standings for the year and marked him as the driver to beat for the remainder of the season. Although Gordon didn't win another race, he continued to run well.

The season was marred by a single incident that also demonstrated the level of respect — and concern — racing with Gordon now brought out in other drivers. During one race Gordon was having a hard time passing driver Ricky Rudd because of trouble with his tires. As the two raced down the track at nearly 200 miles per hour only inches part, Gordon's tires suddenly grabbed and his car lurched slightly to one side, just far enough to graze Rudd's car.

Responsible NASCAR drivers never initiate contact

with another car if there is any way they can prevent it. Racing at such high speeds, even a slight nudge from another car can be enough to cause a serious accident.

Gordon hadn't meant to strike Rudd. It had been an accident and Gordon was relieved when he noticed that it hadn't caused Rudd any trouble. He later described the contact between the two cars as "like you might have kissed your algebra teacher."

But Rudd took another view of the incident. He was incensed, and later in the race bumped Gordon three times from behind, an extremely dangerous maneuver that could have caused each man to lose control.

Fortunately, Gordon was able to maintain control, but the incident underscored how seriously the other drivers now took Gordon on the track. Drivers who have no chance to win are rarely the object of such attention from their peers. But Gordon was a threat to win in every race he entered.

The two drivers sniped at each other after the race. NASCAR threatened to discipline both men, but eventually decided to take no action. Gordon finished the year eighth in the Winston Cup standings behind winner Dale Earnhardt, and won $1.8 million in prize money. The Rainbow Warriors were recognized for their contribution and chosen as the Pit Crew of the Year.

But in the hearts of many NASCAR fans, Gordon was second to no one. Despite his marriage to Brooke at the end of the season, the news of which broke the hearts of female racing fans all over the country, he had become the most popular driver in the Winston Cup Series. A new, younger, more affluent generation of racing fans had been drawn to NASCAR by Gordon, a driver whom they found it easier to identify with. As veteran driver Dale Jarrett told a reporter, "It should be illegal to be that young, that good-looking, and that talented." Advertisers realized that Gordon was something special and he began signing lucrative endorsement deals for cereal and other products. While many NASCAR drivers endorsed automotive products, few had ever been considered popular enough to be used commercially for products aimed at the general consumer. But Gordon was different.

Gordon and his team spent the off-season getting ready for 1995. His first two years on the Winston Cup circuit had served as his apprenticeship. In 1995, everyone on his team, from Gordon and Evernham to car owner Rick Hendrick and Gordon's wife, Brooke, expected him to contend for the Winston Cup title in 1995. As they began the season expectations were high.

But Gordon and his team soon learned that expectations brought no guarantee of success. In order to win, each of them still had to perform their jobs perfectly.

In the season opener, the Daytona 500, Gordon qualified in fourth place in his new car, a Monte Carlo painted in his now-familiar rainbow colors. But once the race began, he surged to the lead and led for more than 50 laps. Midway through the race, Gordon appeared to be in command. Then he came to the pits for a routine stop.

As they had hundreds and hundreds of times before, as soon as Gordon rolled to a stop, his crew went into action — cleaning his windshield and grill, dumping fuel in his tank, and jacking the car up to make a tire change.

But the crew member responsible for changing the front left tire made a critical error, missing a lug nut when he tried to remove the tire. When he pulled on the tire to take it off, the tire refused to budge.

Meanwhile, the jack man scanned the car to make sure the tire changes were done before lowering the car to the track. When he saw the tire changer turn away, he thought that he was finished. He didn't realize that the tire hadn't been changed yet and that the tire changer, realizing that a lug nut remained on the wheel, was reaching back for his air-powered wrench to remove it.

The jack man dropped the car back down to the pavement. As soon as his car hit the ground, Gordon put it in gear and pulled away from the pit.

He only traveled a car length or two before the tire, held in place by a single nut, wiggled and then sheared off the bolt. The wheel rolled free and the left front end of Gordon's car dipped onto the asphalt, sending sparks flying. The fender collapsed under the weight of the car.

Finally realizing their mistake, the crew hurriedly pushed the car back into the pit, jacked the car up again, and surveyed the damage. Although the car was easily repairable, it took some precious time to bend the fender back in place, check for further damage, then replace the tire and send Gordon back onto the track.

While the seconds ticked away, car after car whizzed by on the track. By the time Gordon made it back out, his lead was gone. More than two dozen cars had passed him!

It was too late in the race to make up for the mistake. Although he raced as hard as he could, by the time the checkered flag was waved for winner Sterling Martin, Gordon was still far back in the pack and finished 22nd. "We just gave the race away," moaned Evernham afterward. "It's just a shame."

The miscue served as a wake-up call for the reigning Pit Crew of the Year. In the next race, they were determined not to make a mistake.

They didn't. At the Goodwrench 500, Gordon won the pole. When the race began he charged to the front. He led for more than half the race. The Rainbow Warriors performed flawlessly, giving Gordon the precious advantage of gaining a second or two on the field every time he entered the pits. He won the race going away.

Although a broken fuel pump knocked him out early in the next race, in the following race, the Purolator 500, Gordon absolutely destroyed the entire field, at times leading by a remarkable 17 seconds. In a sport where the first- and second-place cars are often separated by hundredths, or even thousandths, of a second, a 17-second lead is almost beyond belief. Gordon's new Monte Carlo and his team were working in perfect unison.

About the only thing that could stop him were things out of his control, like accidents. After winning the pole for the third time of the season and leading the TranSouth 400, Gordon ran into trouble when another driver spun out ahead of him. He was blocked on both sides and couldn't avoid an accident. He plowed into another car. Fortunately, neither Gordon nor any of the other drivers were seriously hurt, but Gordon was knocked from the race.

His crew worked overtime to repair the car for the next race, and they performed their task to perfection. Gordon won the Food City 500, then finished second, third, second, and third again in the next four races. Thus far in the season, Gordon and Dale Earnhardt had dominated, and they shared the Winston Cup lead.

Both men drove Chevrolets. NASCAR worried that the cars might have an unfair advantage. They ordered everyone driving Chevys to make a small change in their spoilers, the small wing on the rear of the car that helps hold it to the track. At the same time, they allowed drivers of other makes of car to make improvements in their spoilers.

The change made the races more competitive, and it took Gordon and his crew several races to adapt. When they did, it was back to victory lane.

In his next thirteen races, Gordon finished in the top ten every time, and in the top three a remarkable eight times, including four more victories.

But everything wasn't quite perfect. In the Die Hard 500, Gordon made a mistake that could have turned tragic. While working to pass driver Kenny Schrader, Gordon lost traction and his front fender banged into Schrader's car.

That was enough to send Schrader sideways,

causing driver Ricky Craven to strike the rear of Schrader's car.

Gordon was in front of the accident and could do nothing but watch in horror through his rearview mirror as Schrader's car became airborne. It tumbled and twisted through the air and up against the wall. The caution flag came out immediately and Gordon slowed, worried sick that he might have inadvertently caused injury to another driver.

For a few tense moments, as Gordon said later, "it was very scary." But he soon heard a familiar voice on his radio — Kenny Schrader.

"I've never met anybody like Schrader," Gordon admitted after the race. "Most guys you put in the wall are waiting to punch you out, but he was on my radio assuring me he wasn't upset with me. It was a mistake on my part and I hope it never happens again." As every driver knew, accidents were a part of racing, and although each driver usually does his best to avoid them, it's impossible to do so all the time.

Entering the final race of the season, Gordon held a narrow lead over Dale Earnhardt for the Winston Cup championship. But his victory still wasn't assured. If Earnhardt won the race, and Gordon was forced from the race by a mechanical failure or accident, Earnhardt could still win the title.

Knowing he needed to win, Earnhardt raced aggressively and bolted to the lead. Gordon, meanwhile, was hampered by some small mechanical problems and fell back. Knowing he couldn't win the race, but also aware that he needed to finish in order to win the Winston Cup title, he raced smart and stayed out of trouble. Although Earnhardt won, and Gordon finished 16 laps back in 32nd place, he did exactly what he needed to do.

At age twenty-four, Gordon became the Winston Cup champion, the second-youngest driver ever to capture the title. With seven wins Gordon earned more than four million dollars, including a bonus of nearly two million for winning the title.

His victory made him familiar even to non–racing fans. He made a number of television appearances on programs like *Good Morning America* and the *Late Show with David Letterman*. For the year-end NASCAR banquet, Rick Hendrick chartered a plane and flew a total of one hundred sixty people to the event.

Gordon was magnanimous in victory, praising Earnhardt and giving most of the credit to others — the Rainbow Warriors, his family, and Hendrick, later saying, "Winning the title is just too good to be true."

That's just what people were saying about Gordon. So far, his career had been too good to be true. His challenge now was to answer the question of whether he could maintain his lofty standing.

Chapter Nine:
1996–1997

Back on Top

Despite Gordon's remarkable 1995 season, some NASCAR insiders, like the writers who covered the sport, and some jealous drivers, considered his performance a fluke. They still thought he was a spoiled kid who had grown up with every advantage, ignoring all the hard work that went into his racing effort. They pointed to the success of the other Hendrick drivers, most notably Terry Labonte, and charged that Gordon was just the beneficiary of the dominance of the Hendrick team. Anyone could win driving for Hendrick, they sniped. In a preseason poll, fewer than 10 percent of the journalists covering the Winston Cup thought Gordon would repeat as champion.

Gordon gave his critics plenty of fuel in the first two races of the season, the Daytona 500 and the

Goodwrench 400. Only eight laps into Daytona, Gordon got squeezed and banged hard against the wall.

Most drivers would have withdrawn from the race, but Gordon's team worked feverishly on his car. Nearly two hours later, after more than 100 laps had been run, Gordon went back on the track and attempted to finish. But the car wouldn't respond properly and he reluctantly pulled out. He finished in 42nd place — dead last, his worst finish ever as a driver at any level.

There was nowhere to go but up — almost. For in the Goodwrench 400, Gordon blew an engine soon after the start. He finished 40th, in last place for the second week in a row.

According to the scoring system used to determine the Winston Cup champion, each driver receives a certain number of points based upon their finish in a given race. On the whole, the system rewards drivers who contend from week to week, favoring consistency over the occasional brilliant win. By finishing last two weeks in a row, chances were slim that Gordon could still win the points championship. Dale Earnhardt had already finished first and second in the same two races. To catch him, Gordon would have to start winning, or coming very close, almost every week.

He snapped out of his doldrums in the next race, the Pontiac 400. In a race marred by a series of accidents and caution flags, Gordon stayed patient, nailed a restart perfectly, and with only a few laps to go zoomed ahead, stealing a victory with a consummate example of his driving skill.

The victory spurred him to two more wins and three more top-three finishes in the next five races. But at Talledega in the Winston Select 500, Gordon experienced the worst accident of his career.

As he jockeyed for position near the front, Sterling Marlin bumped Dale Earnhardt into the wall. Earnhardt's car spun crazily across the track, and car after car following in his wake got caught up in the chain reaction.

As car parts and tires flew through the air all around him, Gordon smashed into Earnhardt. "I just closed my eyes," Gordon said later, "and kept hearing, 'Boom,'" as his car was struck again and again by debris. Fortunately, no one was seriously hurt, but nine cars, including Gordon's number 24, were knocked from the race.

His team quickly rebounded, but every five or six races something bad would happen early in the race. Gordon would finish far back, costing him vital points in the battle for the season championship.

However, late in the season, he put together the greatest streak of his brief NASCAR career. In consecutive weeks, he finished second, first, second, and then won three races in a row to bring his victory total to an astounding ten for the season. But, in the Quality 500 in Charlotte, bad luck struck again. His engine overheated and the resulting long pit stop knocked him from contention. Gordon finished 31st while teammate Terry Labonte, who seemed to spend the whole year racing just behind the leaders, won his first race of the season. Labonte's consistency pulled him just ahead of Gordon in the points race.

In the final three races of the year, Gordon's good luck ran out while his misfortune continued. In each race, small problems marred otherwise successful runs. He finished twelfth, fifth, and third. Despite the fact that Gordon won a total of ten races to Labonte's two, and that each man had finished in the top five an incredible 21 times in 31 starts, Gordon's last-place finishes at the start of the season had hurt him. Labonte was able to nose him out for the title.

Gordon was disappointed at not winning the Winston Cup, but he also knew he'd silenced the critics who said he was a one-year wonder. Well, they hadn't really been silenced. At nearly every race, Gordon was greeted with a cacophony of boos, as NASCAR fans had split into two camps, one made up of those who supported Gordon and a more vociferous group who resented him and let him know it.

Gordon didn't let the jeers affect him. He knew that behind them there was actually a grudging kind of respect. He had to be a pretty good driver in order to get fans so worked up. And that was good for racing.

As if Gordon needed any further motivation in 1997, just as the season started he learned that Rick Hendrick was ill with a dangerous form of leukemia, a blood disease. It was the second time the disease had struck the team. Several years before, Ray Evernham's son had also contracted leukemia. Hendrick had paid for the boy's medical care. Gordon was close to the car owner and was determined to prove his loyalty on the track.

At Daytona, Gordon's car displayed "1-800-MARROW-2," the telephone number of a charity that was fighting Hendrick's disease. Every time Gordon led a race or crossed the finish line in 1997, he knew he was helping his boss by giving the disease that afflicted him more attention.

Of all the honors Gordon had won in his brief career, only one still eluded him. He had never won the Daytona 500, NASCAR's equivalent of the Super Bowl or World Series, the race Dale Earnhardt termed "the granddaddy of them all." He wanted badly to win the race, both for Hendrick and for himself.

Early in the race, Gordon stormed to the lead. But on lap 110, he cut a tire and had to make an unscheduled and costly pit stop to have it replaced while the other cars were running under the green flag. Whenever possible, NASCAR drivers try to avoid unscheduled pit stops, particularly under the green flag. While they're siting motionless in the pits, the rest of the field is whizzing past at almost 200 miles per hour. It is virtually impossible to recover after such an unscheduled stop.

But the Rainbow Warriors did their job to perfection and got Gordon back on the track before he'd been lapped by the leaders. He was still far behind, but at least he was on the same lap.

Then he got lucky. A yellow caution flag came out and the field became bunched up again. During a yellow, cars aren't allowed to pass each other, but gaps between cars evaporate as everyone runs together in a group. Now Gordon had a chance.

When the green flag came out again, he picked his way patiently through the field. When Dale Earnhardt left the race after an accident, Gordon and his two Hendrick teammates, Terry Labonte and Ricky Craven, were one-two-three behind leader Bill Elliott.

A driver has a tremendous advantage when running together with his teammates. Although each individual is out to win, teammates tend to work together to help each other out, creating drafts for one another.

With only a few laps remaining, Gordon radioed Labonte and said, "It would be pretty cool if we could get these three Hendrick cars past Elliott." Labonte agreed, as did Craven when Gordon contacted him a few moments later. A one-two-three finish for Hendrick cars would be the best present the three drivers could give to the leader of their team.

With Gordon running in second place, Labonte and Craven lined up neatly behind him with only inches separating the three cars. In such a configuration, the effects of drafting are enhanced. Gordon, in the lead car, carved a virtual tunnel through the air. With Labonte and Craven lined up so closely behind him, he, in turn, received a bit of a push as they cut down on the drag created by the turbulent air.

Just ahead of the three men, Bill Elliott looked into his rearview mirror and his heart sank. With the finish line almost in sight, he knew what was about to happen.

The effects of drafting allowed each of the three

Hendrick drivers to run several precious miles an hour faster than Elliott. Coming out of a turn, Gordon dropped to the inside and his teammates followed. Elliott watched helplessly as the three passed him like he was driving in the slow lane on the interstate.

Moments later the three drivers surged across the finish line, first, second, and third. Never before had three teammates finished in the top three in the same race. And to have it happen at Daytona made it even better.

As soon as he got to the victory lane, Gordon grabbed a cell phone and called Hendrick, who was too ill to attend the race. "We love you. This one's for you," he shouted. Gordon was the youngest winner ever at Daytona.

Gordon followed his big Daytona win with another in the Goodwrench 400, giving him a commanding lead in the points race. This time, he wouldn't have to start from the back of the pack.

That still didn't mean it would be easy. NASCAR officials, again concerned that Chevrolets driven by Gordon and the rest of the Hendrick team had an unfair advantage, soon made a rule change that allowed the Fords and Pontiacs to increase the size of their rear spoiler. Gordon didn't think it was fair, but he didn't complain.

The change worked. Fords and Pontiacs suddenly began winning races, while the Chevys started to struggle — except for Jeff Gordon's number 24. The rule change didn't seem to affect him one bit. In a stretch of 18 races, Fords and Pontiacs driven by various drivers won 11 times. A Chevy driven by Jeff Gordon won the other seven!

With only one race remaining in the season, Gordon clung to a narrow lead in the points race. After racing superbly for much of the year, another run of bad luck had hurt him and allowed drivers Dale Jarrett and Mark Martin to draw close. In the NAPA 500, Gordon had to finish in the top 18 to guarantee another Winston Cup championship. If he did that, he'd win, even if Jarrett or Martin won the race.

Normally, that would make Gordon confident, but during the practice run he spun out while coming into the pits. The team hurriedly removed the engine and worked all night to install it in his backup car. He barely qualified for the race, starting in 37th place. The car wasn't running very well. All of a sudden finishing in the top 18 looked like a long-shot. He knew that winning the race was out of the question.

It is easy for a driver when his car is working well. But the real test of a driver's skill can often be measured by how well he races when his car isn't the best in the field. That's when his own skills come to the fore.

The effect of the trouble Gordon was having with his car showed up in tire wear. The car was loose and wouldn't hold a line very well, which resulted in his tires wearing down much faster than usual. With only 56 laps remaining, Gordon was forced into the pits for a tire change.

He hadn't been able to squeeze 50 laps from a set of tires all day, but he knew that if he came into the pits for another change he could kiss the Winston Cup championship good-bye. Martin was leading and Jarrett was running close to the lead. After consulting with Ray Evernham, Gordon decided to take a chance. He would run the remainder of the race on the same four tires.

He charged out of the pits and found his way onto the track in 19th place, where he desperately tried to find a clean racing line. At first, the new tires held him firm, but as they wore down a bit more with each revolution of the track, he felt his car becoming looser and looser. Every turn he entered became an adventure as the car began to slip and slide on the oil-covered track.

The remainder of the race would be a test of Gordon's driving skills, and a big one. If he backed off, he would lose the championship. But if he raced too hard, he would crash and still lose the championship. Somewhere on the track was the fine line that meant the difference between victory and defeat. Somehow, Gordon had to find it.

His tires were worn down to the cords. Driving on them was like driving on ice — at about 200 miles per hour!

But this was an instance where Gordon's twenty-plus years of racing, starting at age five, paid off. He had driven so many races in so many different cars under so many conditions that he felt as if he could feel the surface of his own tires as they tried to find a grip on the track. Somehow, he managed to both maintain his speed and keep his car on the track.

It was "white-knuckle" driving at its best, just a car and a driver demanding the most out of each other.

For Gordon, the last few minutes of the race went by excruciatingly slow. Finally, on the last lap, he came out of turn four clean and saw the checkered flag far ahead waving the winner of the race — Terry LaBonte — into victory lane. Jarrett finished second and Martin third.

Gordon let out a big sigh of relief and aimed his car straight down the track toward the finish, ending the race in 17th place, edging out Jarrett by only 14 points to win the Winston Cup championship.

Gordon's team was jubilant at the end of the race. No driver had ever been happier to finish 17th! And, to his surprise, he heard an unfamiliar sound from the 160,000 fans in attendance. When the track announcer informed them that Gordon had hung on to win the championship, they cheered him long and loud, knowing that he had driven one of the best races of his career just to finish 17th.

"I think," said Gordon, grinning broadly as he listened to the crowd, "they respect the Winston Cup champion."

Chapter Ten:
1998-1999

Racing Ahead

Gordon was right. His victory had demonstrated to everyone that the most important factor in his success was his talent. Besides, after five years of Winston Cup racing, he wasn't "the Kid" anymore. He was a veteran.

Incredibly, after only five years, he was already among the top twenty NASCAR drivers of all-time in career wins. Although Richard Petty's 200 career wins were a long way off, it was becoming clear that if anyone was every going to challenge that mark, it would be Gordon. In a sense, his only competition from here on would be himself — and history.

After a slow start in 1998, Gordon got going in midseason, finishing in the top five in an incredible 17 consecutive races. Far from being satisfied with what he had done in racing, Gordon seemed determined to become even better.

Beginning with the Pennsylvania 500, Gordon proved that his remarkable performance thus far was only the beginning. He followed a victory there with another in the Brickyard 400, winning with a nifty piece of strategic racing that took advantage of a series of caution flags, culminated by a race-ending, five-lap dash to the finish after yet another yellow.

In his next race at the Watkins Glen road course, a winding circuit made up of eleven turns and particularly demanding for stock cars, Gordon again demonstrated why he was the best driver in NASCAR. Running well in midrace, he came into the pits, where the Rainbow Warriors had a rare miscue. By the time he took the track again, he was in 15th place.

But the best driver and the best car were still hard to beat. Gordon weaved through traffic and caught leader Mike Skinner with only three laps to go. Fellow driver Mark Martin summed up Gordon's performance after the race by telling the press, "He [Gordon] gave us a driving lesson. He is just awesome."

Gordon and his team then traveled to the Michigan Speedway looking for a fourth consecutive win. Gordon again caught the leader just before the end of the race.

No NASCAR driver, not even Richard Petty, had ever won five races in a row. All eyes were on Gordon at the start of the Goody's 500.

Unfortunately, if they followed Gordon the entire race, they missed the leader. Car trouble kept him from challenging for the lead, even though he finished in fifth place. But then Gordon followed with two more victories, running his streak to an unbelievable six wins in seven races, and a total of ten for the year.

No one could stop Gordon, although everyone tried. One car owner charged that Gordon's crew was treating his tires with a mysterious illegal substance that was giving them an unfair advantage. NASCAR investigated, but found the charges to be without any basis. Gordon was accustomed to such accusations.

After a string of second-place finishes, Gordon found the victory lane again in the Pepsi 400, then won his 12th race at the AC Delco 400 to clinch the Winston Cup championship. But there was still one race left in the season.

Another driver may well have skipped the race. After all, why risk injury when you already have the title sewn up? But Gordon knew that a win would tie Richard Petty's record of 13 victories in a season.

Like he had done so many times before that season, Gordon hung close for most of the race and closed with a flourish, passing Dale Garrett only six laps from the finish. To Gordon, 13 was a very lucky number.

The way Gordon ended the 1998 season and began 1999, it appeared as if he may never lose again. He started the year winning the Daytona 500 in thrilling fashion.

After securing the pole, Gordon spent most of the race biding his time, saving his car and jockeying for position just behind the leaders. Over the first 187 laps of the race, Gordon had led for a mere six. But with only 13 laps remaining, Gordon decided to make his move.

Trailing both Rusty Wallace and Dale Earnhardt,

Gordon first picked off Earnhardt, then set his sights on the leader, Wallace. He drew to within inches of Wallace's car, then waited for his opportunity. Meanwhile, Earnhardt hadn't given up. He was hoping to follow in Gordon's wake past Wallace, as well.

Entering the first turn of lap 190, Gordon saw his chance. He dropped inside Wallace, then squeezed past a slower car through the turn.

Gordon held his narrow lead down the straightaway, but as he entered turn three, Wallace drew even. Mike Skinner, Earnhardt's teammate, now chose to challenge Wallace from the outside. The cars were three abreast, only inches separating them.

But Gordon just couldn't pull ahead. Then he received some unexpected help.

Dale Earnhardt dropped in behind him. He needed to pass Wallace as well, and knew the only way he could do so would be to help Gordon. The unexpected push was enough to send Gordon past Wallace, and Earnhardt followed in his wake to take second place.

With only ten laps to go, the past and future of

racing had everyone's attention: Earnhardt, a veteran of more than two decades and the defending Daytona 500 champion, versus Gordon, the new kid on the block and the future of the sport.

Fans thrilled as Earnhardt chased Gordon around the racetrack, desperately trying to pass him. Gordon, meanwhile, did all he could to stay ahead of Earnhardt.

Coming out of the final turn on the final lap, Earnhardt made one last try on the straightaway. But he couldn't get any closer than two car lengths. Gordon crossed the finish line and saw the checkered flag. Earnhardt passed the line only 0.128 of a second behind him.

As the two cars slowed, Earnhardt drew even with Gordon, playfully tapped the side of his car and gave him a small wave in salute. After the race, Gordon returned the salute to Earnhardt, saying, "I couldn't have done it without his help. It's a dream come true for me to race Dale Earnhardt all the way to the finish line in the Daytona 500."

But after so much success, the remainder of the 1999 season proved just how tough it is for dreams to come true all the time. Although Gordon won six more races, car trouble and small accidents knocked him from several races early. Sadly, those withdrawals ruined his chance to win an unprecedented third straight Winston Cup championship. He finished sixth, reason to celebrate for most drivers, but a reason for Jeff Gordon to rethink his future.

At the end of the year, Gordon and Ray Evernham decided to go their separate ways. Both had learned and grown much during their years together, and both men wanted to move on. Evernham hoped to put together a new team and find a new challenge, while Gordon purchased an ownership interest in the team and assumed responsibility for running all aspects of it behind his number 24 Monte Carlo.

If Gordon's past is any indication of his future, that can't be good news for other drivers — although it may be very good news for NASCAR. For at each stage of his racing career, after a period of adjustment, Gordon has quickly reached an unmatched level of dominance. There is every reason to believe that Jeff Gordon, driver and owner, will prove to be similarly successful.

Yet despite all his achievements, Gordon has managed to keep everything in perspective. "I'm very fortunate," he told a reporter. "I'm very blessed that my life has turned out this way."

Jeff Gordon's eyes are still focused on finish lines far ahead.

Matt Christopher

Sports Bio Bookshelf

Terrell Davis	Tara Lipinski
John Elway	Mark McGwire
Julie Foudy	Greg Maddux
Wayne Gretzky	Hakeem Olajuwon
Ken Griffey Jr.	Briana Scurry
Mia Hamm	Emmitt Smith
Grant Hill	Sammy Sosa
Derek Jeter	Mo Vaughn
Randy Johnson	Tiger Woods
Michael Jordan	Steve Young
Lisa Leslie	

The #1 Sports Series for Kids

Read them all!

All available in paperback from Little, Brown and Company